your employer sucked.

How to **thrive** through an unexpected **change**

BARRY KING

"Change is the law of life. And those who look only to the past or present are certain to miss the future."
- John F. Kennedy

CONTENTS

INTRODUCTION

Change is inevitable, but it's never easy. Few changes make you want to scream that your "employer sucks!" more than the shocking news of a layoff.

In an instant, lives are disrupted and uncertainty sets in. The ensuing whirlwind of emotions—disbelief, anger, hurt, anxiety—is overwhelming.

If you've picked up this book after cursing your company or even manager's name, you're likely reeling from the hit of a layoff.

First, know that you will get through this. I know this because I have. Second, know that this layoff is not your fault, even if your employer majorly sucks right now.

Companies undergo restructures, relocations, mergers, downsizing, and more for reasons outside an employee's control. The decision was likely impersonal, but the hurt feels personal nonetheless.

The goal of this book is to help you process the emotions, reframe unhelpful thoughts, and take proactive steps to thrive once more.

You'll learn why layoffs happen and why they aren't a reflection of your worth, regardless of how much your employer sucks.

You'll discover how to healthily grieve then emerge stronger. Stories from others will validate your experience and show that you aren't alone.

With tips for leveraging your skills, networks, and core strengths, you'll gain confidence to not just rebound but chart a new course.

Change will keep happening, but you get to choose how to respond. So come along as we transform this layoff from a bruise to a boost.

Once you learn these strategies for harnessing change, you'll be equipped to navigate life's curveballs with resilience.

The layoff may have stung, but it does not define you.

Now let's get started building the next version of your career and reclaiming your power.

The best is yet to come!

CHAPTER ONE

It's Not You, It's Them

Reflection

You contributed valuable skills, tireless work ethic, and immense effort during your time at the company.

Think back on the positive feedback from performance reviews praising your work. Remember the major projects you spearheaded and or contributed to that were delivered successfully.

Think about colleagues who complimented your collaboration and support. You likely have countless emails, slack and or team's messages thanking you for going above and beyond.

When you consider the tangible evidence objectively, you know deep down that you performed well in your role. This layoff is not a reflection of your capabilities or worth ethic.

Layoffs most often occur due to factors entirely unrelated to individual performance. The most common reasons are poor financial outlook, mergers and acquisitions, or overall downsizing.

Entire teams and divisions are often impacted in layoff decisions that are strategic and impersonal.

In fact, your employer may have had to make tough choices about headcount reduction despite recognising your contributions.

Restructuring, outsourcing, and shifting business needs also commonly precipitate layoffs.

So while the situation feels deeply personal, try to remember it was likely just business.

Layoffs have become relatively common over the past few decades, especially during economic downturns.

According to Bureau of Labor statistics, around 1.7 million employees faced layoffs in 2022.

Studies show that 85% of corporate layoffs are for structural rather than performance-related reasons. This hits even the most established and profitable of [1]companies, including:

- Meta: 13%, 11,000 (September 2022)

- Amazon: 3%, 10,000 (November 2022)

- Google: 6%, 12,000 (January 2023)

- Microsoft: 5%, 10,000 (January 2023)

- Spotify: 17%, 1,500 (December 2023)

Even within the industry that supports you finding your next career move, big players like LinkedIn (3% in 2023) have reported cuts.

These numbers and examples validate that you're far from alone in this experience.

So with entire industries and roles disappearing or morphing due to technology shifts, layoffs will likely continue trending.

So do not interpret a layoff as a reflection of your individual worth or potential.

Know that you're part of a large community navigating this together.[1]

---

[1] Layoff statistics sourced from https://layoffs.fyi/

It's Not Personal

It's completely understandable to feel unfairly targeted or to question your self-worth after a layoff. The sense of rejection stings deeply.

You may indeed think your employer or your manager sucks but it won't empower you to move forward.

Doubting your contributions or skills is a natural emotional response and defence mechanism when your environment changes so abruptly.

However, these doubts and feelings of inadequacy do not reflect reality.

While the emotions are valid, do not let yourself be defined by surfaced insecurities. You are so much more than this temporary setback.

Combat those nagging feelings of inadequacy by objectively examining the facts of your performance.

Re-read past performance reviews, recognition emails, and project successes.

Write down quantifiable achievements, customer feedback, and your proudest accomplishments.

Keep an ongoing list of colleagues who valued your work and times you went above expectations.

Let the tangible evidence ground you in reality when emotions distort your self-perception.

Reflect also on the core strengths and values that make you exceptional. Keep the focus on facts rather than feelings.

It's okay to feel rejected or that your contributions were undervalued when laid off.

Allow yourself to process these emotions rather than suppressing them. But also consciously reframe what first felt like a rejection as an unexpected opportunity.

Use the experience to identify your passions and the type of work environment where you can thrive. Treat it as a pivot point to advocate for your value and to take ownership of your career.

With an openness to change and belief in your abilities, you will harness this setback to propel yourself forward.

What's Next?

In this chapter, we validated that the layoff was not a reflection of your worth.

We discussed strategies for processing difficult emotions without letting them undermine your self-confidence.

Most importantly, we began the journey of reframing this challenge as an opportunity to take control of your career.

Now, give yourself permission to visualise the type of work environment and role where you can thrive.

Reflect on your core strengths and values to chart a course aligned with your passions.

Recognise this transition period as a rare gift to get very clear on what you desire next, without limitations.

It won't happen overnight, but keep taking it one day at a time.

Honour emotions as they arise while also focusing energy on productive planning and self-care.

Avoid ruminating on the past or clinging to resentment. You have so much to offer the right employer.

In Chapter Two, we'll build on these foundations by diving into proven techniques for fostering resilience, adaptability, and calm during even the most turbulent changes.

For now, know that the layoff does not define you. Your journey is just beginning.

CHAPTER TWO

Grieve, Then Thrive

The Emotional Rollercoaster

It's completely normal to experience a rollercoaster of emotions after a layoff.

In order to thrive, sometimes you just need to grieve.

The Kubler-Ross change curve comprises five common stages that people often go through - denial, anger, bargaining, depression, and acceptance.

- Denial: Feelings of shock, disbelief, burying your head.

Tips: Talk to trusted friends, start a journal, look for support groups.

- Anger: Feelings of frustration, lashing out, blaming others.

Tips: Vent safely, exercise, avoid rash decisions, examine roots of anger.

- Bargaining: Trying to negotiate the decision, guilt over what you could've done differently.

Tips: Reflect realistically, focus energy on productive planning.

- Depression: Intense sadness, despair, grief over loss.

Tips: Try therapy, lean on your support system, set small goals, practice self-care.

- Acceptance: Coming to terms with the new reality.

Tips: Embrace the change, use it as a pivot point, focus on your strengths.

You may feel all, some or none of these emotions and there is no "right" way to move through the stages - be patient and don't judge yourself.

Allow the emotions without bypassing them. Recognise it will take time to achieve stability.

Rather than suppressing the wide range of difficult emotions that may arise around the layoff, it is important to find constructive ways to safely release them.

Journaling can help unpack your deepest thoughts and provide an outlet that leads to greater self-awareness and discovery during this transition.

Physical activity like running, sports or exercise can be a healthy channel for any pent-up stress or frustration.

Creative pursuits such as painting, music, or cooking allow you to tap into your emotions through different modalities of expression.

Having heart-to-heart conversations and talking honestly with trusted colleagues, friends or family who will listen without judgment can help enormously.

You may also consider speaking to a professional counsellor or coach who specialises in grief and change management, as they have therapeutic techniques that can guide you in navigating turbulent emotions with more purpose.

Joining support groups can validate that you are not alone in experiencing this wide gamut of emotional reactions to a layoff.

Meditation and mindful movement like yoga or walking can be helpful to calm unhelpful mental rumination and soothe the nervous system when it feels overloaded.

Setting small achievable goals each day provides an sense of control and accomplishment.

Self-care through nourishing foods, social connection, and restorative rest all enable you to face the emotional waves with renewed energy.

Be patient and compassionate with yourself as you process it all - there is no one right timeline.

We hope these suggestions provide a helpful starting point to guide you through to acceptance and beyond.

Survivor's Guilt

As someone who was directly impacted by the layoff, you likely feel as we have discussed a range of emotions - sadness, anger, betrayal, uncertainty.

It may seem impossible to comprehend the perspective of colleagues who remained employed.

However, they may be experiencing their own survivor's guilt.

By considering how it would feel to stay while others lost jobs, you can humanise the situation.

Recognising the guilt and empathy they feel for former peers can help you avoid resentment.

Their fortune does not undermine your worthiness. You both became victims of circumstances outside your control.

Looking through the lens of survivor's guilt can reframe negative feelings into understanding and support for one another during a traumatic event.

Focusing on shared humanity and compassion, rather than divisive blame, can help everyone impacted move forward in a positive way.

You may be on different paths now, but are connected by the shared hardship of the layoff experience.

Let's look through the lens of the fortunate.

Feeling guilty that you kept your job while colleagues and potentially friends lost theirs can often be profound sense of injustice or shame at being spared from the layoff that impacted so many others.

They may replay conversations wondering if they could have done something to change the outcome for you. Or they may feel unworthy, which transforms into pressure to prove their worth.

While these emotions of guilt and responsibility are understandable, recognising that the situation was out of their control is important.

The decisions were or often made at the organisational level, not due to any shortcoming of individual employees.

They should focus their energy on gratitude for what they have rather than regret. Reflect on the talents and skills that they bring, without diminishing the contributions of those less fortunate.

Avoid unhealthy comparison or competition mindsets. Your colleagues' misfortune or fortune is not tied to worth.

There are many meaningful ways to support former colleagues that can transform survivor's guilt into compassionate action.

- They can share job leads and make introductions to your connections.

- Provide references highlighting talents.

- Send encouragement through texts or motivating cards.

- Celebrate contributions and share memories.

But also recognise that your path forward is not their responsibility to fix.

Hopefully, they can find ways to lend support while maintaining healthy boundaries.

Reframe Your Narrative

When stuck in feelings of victimhood or endlessly questioning "why me?", it can be helpful to intentionally reframe your inner narrative. If you find yourself ruminating on the layoff and paralysed by disempowering thoughts, pause and disrupt the pattern.

When I was laid off from my job as an Enterprise Architect, where I had worked for over 10 years, my inner narrative sound like:

"I'm not good enough, that's why I was let go. I must have made a mistake for this to happen to me. I'll never find something as good as what I had."

A feeling of total failure.

That negative narrative threatened to drag me into a downward spiral of depression and erode my confidence. As we have learnt so far throughout this book and something I didn't know at the time, is that this pattern is very common.

I refused to let anxious worries convince me that I wouldn't succeed again.

I re-wrote this narrative, telling myself:

"This layoff was due to restructuring, not my capabilities. My past performance reviews prove my skills are valued. I contributed so much to major initiatives here. I will take all that experience and find a company that appreciates my potential even more. This is just a chance to redirect my career towards what I'm most passionate about. I can do this."

Repeating empowering mantras like "My skills are still relevant" and "I will succeed again", I took control of the story. I focused on transferable accomplishments, not what was lost.

By purposely reframing my inner narrative, I went from victim to a leader of my life.

Write down the negative story looping in your mind. Then ask yourself - is this absolute truth or just my interpretation? What alternative, balanced perspectives could I consider?

Actively reshape your inner narrative to be more constructive. Focus on your strengths and the opportunities this change could unlock.

Write down affirmations of your self-worth and capabilities. When self-doubt creeps in, counter it consciously with grounded facts of your accomplishments.

Surround yourself with those who speak positively into your life. Be mindful of negative self-talk and limit time with toxic influences.

Affirming mantras repeated regularly can be powerful in instilling self-belief, even if you don't fully feel them yet.

Phrases like "I am capable", "My value is unchanged", "I will succeed again" or "This will open new doors" can validate your innate worth.

Over time and with consistency, your actions will align with the empowering narrative.

Allow this period to shape you into an even stronger version of yourself.

"A layoff induced by forces outside individual performance says nothing about a person's talents, commitment, or potential."
- Daniel Goleman, author of Emotional Intelligence

How to Thrive

In this chapter, we covered strategies to healthily grieve the loss of your job, process difficult emotions, and reframe unhelpful narratives.

You heard about my own personal experience and how reframing helped me in realigning my own journey.

Recognise this layoff as just one chapter, not your entire story. Honour the grief to move through it.

Now shift your focus to how you will thrive.

In Chapter Three, we'll discuss skills and knowledge to proactively build during this transition period.

Invest in yourself through courses, credentials, reading, or new hobbies. Embrace the time and space to develop greater self-awareness.

Reflect on what truly matters to you in next steps, without limitations. Get clear on your strengths, values, and passions. Envision the career and life path where you can utilise them fully.

Let this layoff be the catalyst to live more intentionally.

You now have access to more possibilities than ever before. So move forward with hope, purpose, and belief in your ability to succeed again.

Allow any setback to strengthen your resilience. You have so much value to offer - the right opportunity is out there.

Stay committed to your growth, and you will emerge thriving.

CHAPTER THREE

Level Up Your Skills

Assess Your Goals

This period of career transition after a job loss invites invaluable time for self-discovery.

Use it as an opportunity to get very clear on your own goals and motivations so when the next opportunity arises, it moves you towards greater alignment and joy.

Sarah was working in the hospitality industry for over a decade when the COVID-19 pandemic hit. She lost her job as a hotel manager due to the downturn in travel. To navigate this, she leveraged her customer service skills and transitioned into a career in online customer support for a technology company. She used her adaptability and transferable skills to pivot into a different industry successfully.

Takeaway: If you find yourself in a similar situation, identify your transferable skills and explore opportunities in different industries that value those skills. Be open to the idea of a career pivot and be proactive in networking and up-skilling to increase your chances of success.

John was laid off from his corporate marketing job. He had a passion for baking and had been experimenting with different recipes as a hobby. After losing his job, he decided to turn his passion into a business. He started a home-based bakery and gradually expanded to an online store. His small baking venture grew into a successful business.

Takeaway: If you have a passion or a side project that you've always wanted to turn into a business, a job loss could be an opportunity to take the leap. Entrepreneurship comes with risks, but with careful planning and dedication, it can be a rewarding path.

Maria was a teacher at a local school that closed due to declining enrolment. She took the job loss as an opportunity to pursue further education in educational technology and online teaching methods. After completing her courses, she found a new job as an instructional designer for an e-learning platform.

Takeaway: Sometimes, job loss can be an impetus to invest in your education and acquire new skills. Consider retraining or up-skilling in an area with high demand. This can open up new career paths and make you more competitive in the job market.

I was let go from my own job and used the experience and expertise gained from publishing books as a hobby to produce this, hopefully, helpful book. It was as much therapy as anything else.

Takeaway: Take the opportunity learn from what has happened. Help others where you can and remember, you are not alone.

In all these examples, the key takeaway is to remain adaptable, open to change, and proactive in your approach to career reset after a job loss

Conduct an inventory of your skills, talents, interests, values and personality traits. What parts of your work energetically light you up? What types of projects or roles do you thrive in? What cultures and environments bring out your best? Use self-reflection exercises to get clarity.

Make lists of your ideal job characteristics, must-haves versus nice-to-haves. Envision your best-case scenario without self-limiting. This is an opportunity to pivot towards a career or lifestyle more aligned with your passions if desired.

There are two frameworks you can use to help you self-assess and identify your strengths and opportunities to work. The first of these is STAR (Situation, Task, Action, Result)

Situation

• Reflect on your current or recent work experiences.

• Consider both your achievements and challenges. What were the key situations, tasks, or projects you were involved in?

Task

- Define the specific tasks and responsibilities you had in those situations. What were your roles and expectations in those work scenarios?

Action

- Think about the actions you took to fulfil your tasks and responsibilities.

- What skills, qualities, and approaches did you use to accomplish your goals or overcome challenges? Consider the positive attributes and behaviours that contributed to your success.

Result

- Analyse the outcomes of your actions. What were the results of your efforts?

- Did you achieve your objectives? Were there any lessons learned, or areas where you could have improved?

Using this self-assessment technique, you can identify your strengths, such as strong project management, data-driven decision-making, and team collaboration.

You can also recognise opportunities for work, such as improving your ability to work with limited budgets or enhancing your leadership skills.

This analysis can help you focus on your strengths while proactively addressing areas where you can grow and develop in your career.

The second, extremely common, framework that can be used to evaluate your current situations and gain insights into your career development is SWOT (Strengths, Weaknesses, Opportunities and Threats).

Strengths

• Identify your personal and professional strengths. These are the qualities, skills, and resources that give you an advantage in your career.

- Consider what you excel at, what you are passionate about, and where you've had success in the past.

Examples of strengths might include excellent communication skills, leadership abilities, a strong professional network, or expertise in a particular field.

Weaknesses

- Recognise your weaknesses or areas where you need improvement. These are aspects of yourself that could be holding you back or limiting your career growth.

Examples of weaknesses might include a lack of certain technical skills, poor time management, or difficulty in public speaking.

Opportunities

- Explore external opportunities in your field or industry. These are trends, changes, or possibilities that you can leverage to advance your career.

Examples of opportunities could be a growing demand for professionals with a specific skillset, job openings in a particular location, or emerging market trends.

Threats

- Identify external threats or challenges that may affect your career. These are factors beyond your control that could hinder your progress.

Examples of threats might include economic downturns, industry-specific challenges, or increased competition in your field.

By taking stock of your strengths, weaknesses, opportunities, and threats, you gain critical insights into the best next steps.

Recognising external opportunities allows you to align your natural talents with positions poised for growth. Conversely, reflecting on weaknesses reveals skill gaps needing development, while considering potential threats helps you mitigate risks through preparation.

Whilst you can use these independently, I'd recommend combining SWOT and STAR.

Evaluating Situations, Tasks, Actions, and Results of past jobs or projects highlights transferable skills and concrete examples of your strengths in action.

Together, SWOT and STAR offer multilayered insights into crafting your career path.

By leveraging these self-assessment tools, you gain clarity on where you excel and how to further build on your abilities.

The outcome is a highly personalised roadmap guiding you towards more meaningful, aligned work.

While the layoff derailed one path, you now have the gift of time and distance to re-chart your course thoughtfully.

Set an inspiring vision, then work backwards to outline achievable steps towards it. Let your values and purpose guide you to fulfilling work.

Look for common themes in what most excites you. Research job families, growth areas, and companies making an impact you care about.

The period of career transition after a job loss invites invaluable self-discovery. Use it to get very clear on your own goals and motivations so when the next opportunity arises, it moves you towards greater alignment and joy.

Lifelong Learner

Losing your job provides a unique chance to take a step back and objectively assess your skills and knowledge.

Use this transitional period wisely by embracing a learner's mindset and committing to continual growth.

Start by revisiting the career goals you outlined earlier and analysing any skills gaps holding you back from that vision.

Make a list of both hard and soft skills you need to develop. This assessment will point you towards the appropriate educational opportunities to pursue.

I've always enjoyed and embraced continual learning and this certainly has helped me when I lost my job as it can often be the opportunity and kick needed to start something new.

YouTube for me is the lifeblood for learning anything and may work for you to build any skills you may need or want.

You can also look into online training courses, certification programs, workshops, seminars and other continuing education.

Now is the ideal time to devote focus to gaining qualifications that make you more competitive in your industry. Just be sure what you select aligns with your goals.

Reading is another simple yet powerful way to expand your knowledge. Identify books, publications, articles and other resources tied to your professional interests to soak up new concepts and perspectives.

Staying up-to-date on trends, innovations, theories and more in your desired field or industry is invaluable.

Don't neglect the value of transferable skills as well. Consider new hobbies or activities outside of work that allow you to practice skills like public speaking, creativity, project management and more. Picking up diverse interests can also build confidence in your abilities.

Curiosity is key to lifelong learning.

Maintain the self-assessment and improvement orientation you have right now. Continually seek out new ways to absorb information, gain competencies and grow.

This mindset will serve you throughout your career - not just during transitions.

Transition Time

A job loss understandably shifts your daily routines and responsibilities. Be proactive about filling this transitional period with productive activities that continue building relevant experience.

Completing side projects or freelance work in your field helps maintain recency and prevent resume gaps.

Even if unpaid, these efforts demonstrate initiative and allow you to practice current skills.

They can also be shared as work samples when job seeking.

I wrote this book and as you have learn't as therapy for me and to help others through the process.

If your'e reading this then thank you! I wont be a millionaire but every copy helps me as much as it hopefully helps you.

I also put together a Micro SaaS (Software as a Service) which helps people with insights into the company they are going to interview at and help formulate a 90 day plan when for when they get the job.

Again, this is very unlikely to make me much or anything in return but it builds upon and sharpens transferable skills.

I did these things in my transition whilst looking for a job at the same time.

Volunteer opportunities are another way to stay active while between roles. Seek out local nonprofits where you can contribute your expertise and expand your toolkit with new abilities.

Informational interviews are invaluable for research when considering a career pivot. Reach out to professionals working in fields or roles you may be curious about.

Ask to take them to coffee or set up a quick phone call to ask questions and gain insights about their work.

The time between jobs provides chances to strengthen your profile through both professional projects and personal development.

By being smart with your time, you can exit this transition even more skilled, knowledgeable and employable than before.

The key is focusing efforts toward your goals.

CHAPTER FOUR

Network Smarter, Not Harder

"The most valuable thing in your career will be the network of people you build."
- Reid Hoffman, co-founder of LinkedIn

Your Network

In today's job market, networking is invaluable for unlocking new opportunities. While job boards and online applications have their place, referrals, recommendations, and inside connections are still the top sources of hiring.

According to various studies, an estimated 70-80% of jobs are never advertised publicly. Rather, they are filled quietly through someone in the hiring manager's network suggesting a candidate.

I have worked in the recruitment industry for over 17 years and know first hand how connections are important however you discover what is available and what you do next.

Given how critical personal connections are to surfacing hidden job prospects, putting in the effort to cultivate a diverse network significantly increases your chances for employment.

People naturally want to help others in their network succeed. When you build meaningful relationships, you widen the web of individuals keeping an eye out for appropriate openings on your behalf.

A developed network leads directly to previously inaccessible roles.

The first step to networking smarter is taking inventory of your current connections.

Make a list of all individuals you have built relationships with through past jobs, education, activities, and other avenues.

This could include former colleagues, managers, mentors, classmates, organisation members, vendors, clients, friends and more.

Use LinkedIn to lookup past companies and schools and browse connections. The platform can jog your memory on relationships that may have faded.

Take these contacts into a spreadsheet or database with current contact information, where/how you met them, their industry/role, and any distinct details about your relationship.

Look holistically at all the people you've intersected with personally and professionally, both online and in-person.

This exercise will reveal who already comprises your network and surface any noticeable gaps.

With an understanding of your existing network mapped out, you can then craft more targeted strategies for providing value, expanding your reach, and leveraging connections.

Provide Value

Now you have good starting list of connections, think about how you can begin providing value to this network organically.

Providing value should be at the core of your networking efforts. Rather than viewing connections as transactions, focus on cultivating genuine mutual relationships.

Share knowledge and contacts with your network without expecting anything immediate in return.

If a connection mentions they are interested in pivoting their career or learning a new skill, send them helpful articles or introduce them to someone who can offer insights.

Also think about how you can directly help people in your network based on their goals or pain points.

Could you connect them to future employers, provide useful feedback on their projects, or make introductions to expand their professional circle?

Helping others succeed builds genuine goodwill and strengthens your relationships.

When you provide value freely, your network will naturally keep you top of mind for opportunities.

They will go the extra mile to return the favour when you need it as well.

The most powerful networks are built on trust and reciprocity.

Make it a priority to offer assistance and share knowledge with your connections. If your outreach always centres on asking for something, people may come to dread hearing from you.

Focus on cultivating authentic relationships, not transactions.

Be a generous connector who wants to see the whole community thrive. A mindset of contributing value without expectation builds social capital that always pays forward.

Expand Your Reach

Once you've provided value to your core connections, it's time to broaden your network.

Start by connecting with alumni from schools and companies you previously attended or worked for. Fellow alumni often feel an instant camaraderie and want to help each other thrive.

Use LinkedIn, industry directories, and alumni organisation events to find and engage past colleagues.

Attending conferences, trade shows, and local professional association meetings are prime opportunities to meet new contacts.

Come prepared with plenty of business cards to distribute.

Consider designing your card with a QR code that links to your LinkedIn profile or an online portfolio to spark conversation. This allows you to provide interactive information in a memorable way when networking in-person.

Be ready with an elevator pitch that concisely summarises your background, skills, and goals. Follow up after events to build relationships with promising new connections.

Seeking out networking moments can rapidly expand your community.

Volunteering is a great way to expand your network while also gaining new skills.

As we discussed, research nonprofits aligned to your interests and causes you care about. Local volunteer match services can help you find rewarding opportunities. Your contributions will be welcomed by organisations with limited resources.

LinkedIn remains a powerful platform for expanding your digital footprint. Search for professionals in roles, companies, or geographic areas of interest and request connections. Join relevant industry or niche groups to connect with engaged members.

Again, provide value in all networking scenarios by sharing advice, offering help, and building authentic relationships. Soon your first-level connections will rapidly multiply.

The wider and more diverse your network, the greater potential for uncovering previously unknown job leads and introductions.

Providing value and expanding your network fuel one another in a virtuous cycle.

The wider and more diverse your network the more this allows you to help more people, assisting others earns their trust and grows your footprint.

So maintain a growth mindset and continue expanding your circle.

Lean on Your Network

Once you've built up goodwill and connections, don't be afraid to lean on your network for support and opportunities.

First, identify companies or roles of interest and ask respected contacts if they can facilitate introductions or provide referrals.

Especially turn to connections who work in your target industry or organisation. A personal recommendation gives you an advantage over cold applicants.

When I was looking for my next role, I had ex-colleagues who had connections I hadn't considered. They reached out on my behalf and this provided valuable leads and future connections of my own.

Your network is also invaluable for sourcing informational interviews.

Reach out to experienced professionals in appealing career paths and ask if they would be open to a quick call to provide advice.

Most will be happy to help a fellow connection advance their career through mentorship.

- Be clear and specific when utilising your network.

- Let your goals and ideal next roles be known.

The more details you can provide about your skills, interests, and aspirations the better.

Having explicit conversations clarifies how your contacts may be able to assist you. People genuinely want to help but need to understand exactly where you are headed.

Approach network support as an opportunity, not an obligation.

Here's my top 5 suggestions.

1. Attend alumni and industry events to reconnect with people who have not seen in

some time. People from earlier in your career may have expanded their influence and be able to aid your search.

2.   Don't just ask for job leads. Seek career advice, resume feedback, mock interviews, and mentoring as well. Your network can provide support beyond direct referrals.

3.   Research companies you're interested in and look for any connections working there, even indirectly. Ask them for insights about the workplace culture and values.

4.   When an opportunity arises through your network, ensure you put your best foot forward. Their reputation is on the line for referring you as well.

5.   Scale your asks based on the closeness of the relationship. More frequent or intense favours are better suited for your inner circle of connections.

Contributing value upfront and reinforcing connections builds the goodwill needed for people to eagerly extend a hand during your transition.

Show Appreciation

After someone has connected you with information or opportunities, always follow up to express genuine appreciation.

Send a thank you message, email, or hand-written card. Be specific about what the person did that was helpful and the positive impact it had for you. People want to know their efforts made a difference.

Provide updates on your progress after initial networking interactions.

If an informational interview provided useful insights that guided your job search, let them know. People will feel invested in your career journey when you share outcomes.

Look for chances to return favours and complete the cycle of goodwill.

Introduce former colleagues to new professional contacts that may be beneficial.

Share an interesting article or business idea with a mentor who assisted you.

Also, pay it forward by helping the next person looking to connect. Mentor a junior colleague or volunteer your time to aid those undergoing transitions.

Showing appreciation and returning value cements strong reciprocal relationships for the long haul.

Discovering and landing opportunities relies heavily on others expending their social capital on your behalf.

Always express thanks and follow through on connections provided to you.

Nurturing Connections

The work of networking doesn't end once you've landed a new job. Ongoing nurturing of your connections is crucial.

It takes effort to build this habit, but it will feel more natural over time, even if communication hasn't been your strong suit previously.

Don't just reach out when you need something - this can come across as inauthentic or insincere.

Continue engaging with your network regularly by sharing relevant articles, providing support, and seeing how you can add value.

For newer connections made during your job search, follow up periodically to strengthen the relationship.

1. Set calendar reminders to check in every 2-3 months so you remember to nurture the new connection.

2. Send them articles or resources related to topics you previously discussed that they

found interesting. This shows you listened and remembered.

3. Congratulate them on any major accomplishments like a promotion or new job. Finding excuses to celebrate them builds rapport.

4. Introduce them to other contacts who have complementary interests or expertise. Making connections between your connections strengthens the network.

5. Ask thoughtful questions about how their career, business, or goals are progressing. Then offer your assistance or ideas if any needs arise.

Also remember to give attention to past colleagues and acquaintances from earlier in your career.

Check in to catch up and recap mutual contacts that may be helpful to each other now.

Consider forming an alumni networking group or mastermind collective with fellow ex-coworkers. This creates built-in community support.

Treat networking as a lifelong endeavour that fuels your success and well-being.

Your network will thrive when all feel supported.

CHAPTER FIVE

Ace the Interview (Again)

Reframe Your Mindset

It's common to feel discouraged at having to interview and prove yourself all over again.

But rather than seeing this as starting over, adopt a growth mindset that you're levelling up.

In video games, when players gain enough experience points, they "level up" - upgrading their abilities and power. Levelling up allows them to take on more difficult game challenges.

Similarly, view the period after a layoff as a chance to gain "experience points" for your career. Taking courses, networking, learning new skills are all ways to boost your XP.

Now interviews are an opportunity to show you've levelled up as a candidate. You don't have to start over at level 1. Thanks to your efforts, you now bring a more advanced and well-rounded skillset to the table.

You are like a character that has put in the grind and levelled up before taking on formidable new bosses and quests. Show confidence that all the recent XP you've gained makes you ready to succeed in bigger roles and at new organisations.

The key mindset shift is recognising interviews as a chance to demonstrate your growth and expanded capabilities, not just repeat entry-level basics.

Your previous professional experiences, networking efforts, and continual learning during the transition have equipped you with expanded skills and knowledge. See interviewing as an opportunity to highlight this progression.

Approach the process with confidence in the unique value you now offer. The combination of your established track record and newly strengthened abilities makes you an even more attractive candidate than before.

While you may need to showcase basic qualifications again, emphasise how your profile has become more well-rounded. Use interviews to articulate the deeper experience and distinctive offerings you bring compared to competitors.

The hiring process is a chance to communicate your personal and professional evolution. Be proud of how much you've grown during this transitional period. Develop talking points that convey your readiness to take on greater challenges and responsibilities in this next career stage.

With a levelling-up perspective, interviews become a welcome chance to broadcast the powerful upgrades you've made.

Remember, you have done this before, succeeded and this time you will have the super powers to fly through stronger!

Review Your Story

A key part of preparation is strategically updating your resume and crafting your explanation for leaving your last role.

Take time to carefully update your resume to put your best foot forward.

Lead with a strong branding statement or summary section that conveys your value proposition.

Draw out relevant achievements, projects, skills and competencies from your experience and highlight these prominently.

Check if you can add any new certifications, training programs or education obtained recently to showcase continuous learning.

Remember to tailor your resume and emphasis specifically for each role you are applying to.

This is probably one of the most important tactics to be seen by employers; recruitment systems have sophisticated matching algorithms including the use of AI that will recommend and boost specific profiles to jobs.

You must ensure its not just a keyword-spam, it has to be as authentic as possible. If you see specific requirements of a role and want your CV, profile to match then weave these into your cover letter, profile and or CV as a narrative that makes sense.

Do not misrepresent yourself ; you will need to remain credible. However, terminology and business language used can often be different so try and match yours to the company you are applying to.

Practice explaining your transition from your last role in a concise, forward-focused manner.

Convey that you were ready for a new challenge to further stretch your capabilities, or excited to bring your background into a new industry.

If laid off, pivot the conversation to what you have accomplished since then. Share any professional development initiatives, new skills, or certifications you have gained.

The key is emphasising you are poised for greater responsibility and impact in your next opportunity.

In your work summaries, use the STAR method we shared earlier to powerfully demonstrate relevant competencies.

For example, a Software Engineer might have:

"Led overhaul of client-facing order management system to optimise performance. Identified backend bottlenecks through extensive testing and analysis. Proposed migrating to microservices architecture for greater scalability. Spearheaded development of new microservices and API integration with minimal downtime. Resulting system handled 2x more transactions with 50% faster response time"

In this example, the **Situation** is the outdated order management system. The **Task** is optimising its performance. The **Action** is testing, proposing microservices, and leading development. Finally, the **Result** is increased transactions and faster response time.

Choose examples from your experience that showcase problem-solving, leadership, communication and other key strengths needed for the target role.

Quantify your impact and results where possible. This will help convey you have the right abilities to excel.

Tactical Research

Researching the role and company in-depth can give you a leg up in the interview by demonstrating your interest, knowledge, and enthusiasm.

To understand the role, carefully review the job description and requirements. Make notes on the responsibilities, must-have qualifications, skills and competencies sought.

Check the company's website and LinkedIn to get clarity on day-to-day activities. Identify any gaps you may need to address.

Looking at the ideal talent profile is equally important. What type of experience, qualities, credentials, and attributes are they prioritising? Think through how you can convey strength in those areas with specific examples.

Gaining insight into the company's goals, culture and values provides context on the environment and priorities.

Take a look at the company's website for their mission statement, press releases on new initiatives, recent achievements, and culture code.

Follow their social media channels to get a feel for the brand personality and voice.

Talk to any connections who have insight into the company's inner workings.

Incorporating your research findings into the interview by asking thoughtful questions or referencing relevant facts shows the hiring manager you took time to understand what they are looking for and what makes the organisation unique.

The more tailored your preparation, the better.

Practice Common Questions

In any job interview, one of the keys to success is anticipating the questions you might be asked and preparing thoughtful, comprehensive responses.

A powerful way to do this is by looking through the lens of your core duties in your current or previous roles.

Before you can effectively prepare for potential interview questions, you must have a clear understanding of your core duties.

Reflect on your current or most recent job and identify the primary responsibilities and tasks.

Ask yourself:

- What are the main duties of my role?

- Which tasks do I perform regularly?

- What are the expectations of my position within the company?

Once you have a clear understanding of your duties, it's time to analyse them.

This involves breaking down each duty to understand the skills and knowledge required.

For each duty, consider:

• The skills you applied: Did the task require problem-solving, communication, or technical skills?

• The challenges you faced: What obstacles did you encounter, and how did you overcome them?

• The impact of your work: How did your work benefit the team or company?

With this analysis in hand, you can start to anticipate the types of questions you might be asked in an interview.

Interviewers often ask about past experiences to gauge how you might handle similar situations in the future.

Look at the key expectations of the role advertised to further hone in on what will be more important to have that more finessed answer for.

Consider how your core duties relate to potential questions, such as:

- Problem-solving: "Can you give an example of a challenging problem you faced at work and how you solved it?"

- Teamwork: "Describe a situation where you had to collaborate with others to achieve a goal."

- Leadership: "Tell us about a time when you had to lead a project. What was your approach?"

For each question, provide context for your story, describe your responsibility in that situation, explain the steps you took to address the situation and share the outcome of your actions.

If you find this hard, then use the STAR method we have already used to frame this.

Remember, your responses should be concise, clear, and relevant to the question asked.

Practice articulating these responses, ensuring that they highlight your skills and align with the job you're interviewing for.

Outside of industry and role specific questions, you can expect interviewers to have questions about why you left your last role and what you've been focused on since.

Prepare a concise explanation for your departure that focuses on the future. For example, "I was ready for a new challenge" or "I'm excited to use my skills in a new industry." Take time to practice answering smoothly and confidently.

Here's the top, generic, questions that are often asked during interviews.

1. Tell me about yourself. - This open-ended question is usually an icebreaker, allowing you to introduce your professional background and experiences.

2.   What are your strengths and weaknesses? - Employers ask this to gauge self-awareness and honesty, and to understand how your qualities may fit the role.

3.   Why are you interested in this position / company? - This question assesses your motivation and whether you've done your homework about the company and the role.

4.   Where do you see yourself in five years? - Employers are interested in understanding your career aspirations and whether they align with the company's goals.

5.   Can you describe a challenge you've faced and how you dealt with it? - This question is meant to assess your problem-solving and critical-thinking skills.

6.   How do you handle stress and pressure? - This question helps the interviewer understand how you cope with challenging situations.

7.   What is your greatest achievement? - This question allows you to share your successes

and gives the interviewer insight into your potential for future achievements.

8.   How would your previous colleagues describe you? - This is another way to gauge your self-awareness and how you work in a team environment.

There is a often a final question which we will cover in more detail in the next couple of pages.

"Do you have any questions for us?"

This is a chance for you to show your interest in the role and the company, and to determine if it's a good fit for you.

Let's dig a bit deeper into that.

Ask Insightful Questions

The interview is a two-way conversation, so come prepared with smart questions that demonstrate your understanding of the company and role.

We have discussed the need to research both the role and company, now drawing from your research, ask about the organisation's goals, challenges, and future vision:

- "I read about your plans to expand into new markets this year. What major challenges come with that initiative?"

- "What are the 1-2 top priorities you'd want someone in this role to tackle in their first 6 months?"

- "Where do you envision the most growth opportunities for the company over the next 5 years?"

To show your grasp of the role's responsibilities, you can ask:

- "How would you describe the key attributes of someone who excels in this position?"

- "What are the day-to-day critical functions or deliverables you'd want someone in this role to focus on?"

- "What tools and resources would I have access to in order to support hitting the ground running?"

Inquiring about the qualifications of high performers, expected deliverables, and available tools indicates you comprehensively understand what success looks like.

Aim for 2-3 well-thought-out questions that reflect knowledge of the company's strategic priorities and the role's responsibilities.

Smart questions make a strong impression.

When trying to ascertain if the job is the right fit for you, you may consider some of these aspects.

- What are the characteristics of your ideal culture? How would you describe the culture here?

- How would you describe the management style and work philosophy at this company?

- What opportunities are there for professional development and learning new skills?

- How does the team collaborate on projects? Can you describe the workflow?

- How is performance measured and reviewed? What goals/metrics are team members evaluated on?

- Is there flexibility surrounding work schedules/locations? What are the expectations?

- How would you describe the pace of work? Is it fairly fast-moving or more methodical?

- What processes or tools are in place to support work/life balance for employees?

- How does the organisation support diversity, equity and inclusion in the workplace?

- What makes you excited to come to work at this company every day?

Pick some that resonate with you.

Asking insightful questions about the culture, management style, collaboration, flexibility, diversity, and typical pace of work can reveal if the opportunity aligns with your work style, values and priorities.

This helps determine overall fit beyond just qualifications.

Show Gratitude

Interviews are your chance to stand out from the competition. With many qualified candidates applying for roles today, you need to make a stellar first impression.

Following up after the interview is critical to stay top of mind. If you are able to, send each interviewer a thank you email within 24 hours while it's fresh.

Make sure to personalise this with something specific you discussed. This shows you paid close attention and are genuinely interested.

For example:

"Thank you for taking the time to interview me yesterday for the Project Manager role. It was great learning more about the plans to scale operations over the next year. I'm confident my background managing cross-functional teams and overseeing large product launches can support those growth initiatives. I thoroughly enjoyed our conversation and am very

interested in the opportunity. Please let me know if I can provide any other information."

Personalising with something unique to your conversation demonstrates genuine interest and attention to detail. It also enables you to reinforce examples of your qualifications.

Keep thank you notes concise but add a human touch by highlighting something you connected on.

Whilst it's not always possible depending on the route you have taken to get the interview, a thoughtful follow up can differentiate you as a candidate.

Evaluate And Improve

Interviewing is a skill that can always be honed and enhanced over time through purposeful evaluation and improvement.

Make it a priority after each interview to spend time assessing what went well and where you can upgrade your approach for next time.

Reflect honestly on how you delivered your responses. Did you convey the right energy and confidence? Were your examples compelling and easy to follow? Did you effectively weave in key selling points about your background? Identify areas of strength to continue leveraging.

Also consider what you would refine. Were there certain questions you felt flustered by? Are there gaps in your examples for key requirements? Could your storytelling be tighter or clearer? Make notes on specific areas to work on.

If you have access to feedback from the interviewers, this can provide invaluable insight into how you are perceived. Take any constructive criticism in stride rather than defensively.

Use the lessons learned to focus your preparation and practice for the next opportunity.

Continue polishing your interview skills over time and you will become a confident, compelling candidate.

The more you put yourself out there, the more comfortable the process will become.

Approach each interview experience as a valuable chance to evaluate and upgrade your skills, stories and style.

Commit to continuous improvement and you will see positive results over the trajectory of your career.

Good luck on acing your next interview!

CHAPTER SIX

Chart Your Own Course

Reflect On Your Goals

After experiencing an unexpected transition, it's understandable to feel overwhelmed or stuck. But this final chapter will guide you in taking control to intentionally chart your ideal course forward.

Leveraging all the strategies we've covered - thoughtful reflection, expanding your skills, networking smarter, and acing interviews - you now have the tools to redirect your career towards greater purpose and fulfilment.

While the path may not be linear, in fact you could say it's very squiggly; by staying resilient and open to possibilities, you can navigate this change as a catalyst for positive growth.

Let's look at proactive steps for maintaining momentum on the journey ahead.

This career transition is a pivotal moment to get very clear on your own goals, motivations and ideal working conditions.

Take time to revisit the vision you outlined back in Chapter Three by conducting a personal inventory.

Make lists of your strengths, passions, values and personality attributes. What types of projects energise you? When do you feel in flow?

Assess your working style - do you thrive with structure or flexibility? Collaborating on a team or working independently? Think through your ideal environment.

Envision your best-case scenario for work without limiting yourself. If you could design the role and company culture from scratch, what would it look like? Outline your dream position incorporating your strengths and passions.

Getting clarity on your drivers will help ensure your next step aligns with greater purpose, not just a pile of cash. Don't just default to what you're used to - be open to exploring new directions.

Perhaps this transition is a chance to pursue something you've always been curious about but felt confined by your previous path. Let your values and fulfilment take priority in decision making.

The more clarity you gain through introspection, the easier it will be to identify opportunities that are the right fit after this layoff.

This self-discovery will serve you well beyond just the job search.

Research New Possibilities

After reflecting on your passions, strengths, and goals, conduct research to uncover potential new directions.

Explore growing fields or emerging roles related to your interests.

For example, if you enjoy being creative, look into multimedia roles like animation, podcasting, or video production. The rise of remote work has also opened new niche job categories.

Consider lateral moves into related industries or functional areas. Transferable skills like communication, analysis, and project management are valued across sectors.

A sales professional could pivot into recruitment, a teacher transition into corporate training, and so on.

Seek out companies whose mission or impact resonates with you.

Research "best places to work" rankings and look for organisations giving back to causes you care about. Finding meaning and purpose in your work provides lasting fulfilment.

Conversations with your network, informational interviews, job search platforms, and general exploration of labor market trends can uncover promising new trajectories.

With an open mindset, many possibilities exist.

The transition period empowers you to take informed risks and get creative.

Don't limit your thinking to linear moves. Reflect, research, test out ideas, and then craft your customised career plan.

Craft Your Story

Carefully craft how you present your background when pursuing new directions.

Emphasise transferable abilities that apply across roles and your capacity to quickly learn new skills.

For example, stress your analytical mindset, collaborative nature, and knack for simplifying complex concepts.

Quantifying past achievements also grabs attention.

For instance, rather than just saying "improved sales," share the exact percentage gains you drove. Back general claims with cold hard facts and data.

Convey your passion in your materials and talking points.

Explain why you are energised by aspects of the target company, role, industry, or business challenge. Hiring managers want to see genuine excitement.

Customise your resume, LinkedIn profile, and interview answers for each application rather than taking a one-size-fits-all approach.

Connect your story explicitly to the details in the job description. This tailored focus establishes fit.

Strategic messaging that highlights your transferable value, quantifiable wins, and authentic passion makes your case to transition roles stand out.

Momentum

Persistence is key to managing the ups and downs of the process. Leverage your network for new leads and moral support during challenging times.

Also prepare thoroughly for each interview to boost confidence.

Research the company, role, interviewers, and industry trends so you can knowledgeably discuss these topics.

Rehearse answers to expected questions and polish your professional presentation. Thoughtful preparation reduces anxiety.

Consider short-term transitional roles to build relevant experience if necessary.

For example, if pivoting into a new field, volunteer, pursue a certification, or accept a temporary gig that allows you to demonstrate competencies from that world.

Momentum fuels motivation.

Set Weekly job search goals to keep yourself accountable.

Celebrate small wins like landing an interview or informational meeting.

Maintain positivity and keep sight of your end goal through consistent action.

With determination and focus, you will achieve breakthroughs. Stay the course and make steady progress.

Stay Resilient And Adaptable

Navigating career changes requires bouncing back from disappointments and having an open mind.

When facing rejections or false starts, persist by believing in your inherent worth and abilities. Keep going through the ups and downs, learning along the way.

With resilience, you will eventually achieve the right fit.

Remain open to unorthodox development pathways like lateral moves, entrepreneurship, contract roles, or unconventional companies.

Constraints can spark creativity. Focus less on traditional structures and more on pursuing work you find meaningful and energising.

Lastly, embrace fluidity. Change is the only constant over the course of a career.

View periods of transition as opportunities for self-reflection and growth. Commit to lifelong learning and regularly evaluate your priorities. With adaptability, you can pivot successfully whenever the need arises.

Though the job search journey has challenges, staying positive, determined, and flexible will serve you well.

Keep sight of the expanding possibilities and trust the detours will lead you where you need to go.

AFTERWORD

As you have learnt, charting your own course requires resilience, adaptability, and belief in your inherent worth.

Setbacks and closed doors will happen, but use them to get clearer on your non-negotiables.

Remember, no one can define your value except you.

By combining self-belief with proactive efforts, you will find the right opportunities over time.

This layoff does not limit what you can accomplish. In fact, it can be the start of pursuing work that utilises your strengths and passions in new ways.

With the guidance in this book, you now have strategies to process change, expand your capabilities, and take control of your career journey moving forward.

Stay confident in your value. Believe in your potential. And embrace this transition as a springboard to purposeful work and a life aligned with your unique gifts.

You still may feel your employer sucks by the end of this book but I hope you have been able to see a positive way forward through the uncertainty.

You've got this! Go thrive through this unexpected change.

About the Author

With over two decades helping companies and professionals navigate change, Barry King offers an empowering guide to thriving in times of transition.

Drawing on his extensive experience supporting individuals through layoffs and career pivots, he provides a practical roadmap for processing upheaval, taking control, and emerging stronger.

Blending empathetic storytelling and uplifting advice, this book helps readers transform life's curveballs into catalysts for purposeful growth.

Ideal for anyone dealing with unexpected change in their career or life, it's a reassuring resource for building resilience, optimism and vision to take the next step in your journey.

Printed in Great Britain
by Amazon

37719795R10076